THE MODERN LADIES' COMPENDIUM

JO NESBITT

VIRAGO

This book is respectfully dedicated
to my beloved friend
and ex-flatmate
KEIR WICKENHAM
(the Pittsburgh Nightingale)
who is Not Like another...

JO NESBITT was born in Northumberland in 1949. She was educated at the Convent of the Sacred Heart Grammar School in Newcastle-upon-Tyne and at University College London: the legacies of both institutions are the stuff of divine send-up. Her cartoons and illustrations have appeared in innumerable publications including *Sourcream*, *Spare Rib*, *New Statesman*, *Time Out*, *Undercurrents*, *Honey* and *Feminist Review*. Her children's book, *The Great Escape of Doreen Potts*, was published in 1981. She now lives and works in Amsterdam.

Published by Virago Press Limited 1986
41 William IV Street, London WC2N 4DB

Copyright © Jo Nesbitt 1986

British Library Cataloguing in Publication Data
Nesbitt, Jo
    The modern ladies' compendium
    1. English wit and humour, Pictorial
    I. Title
    741.5'942   NC1479
    ISBN 0-86068-694-9

Printed in Great Britain by Whitstable Litho at Whitstable, Kent

ETIQUETTE

...first aid
for the
vulgar....

...as used
by the
crowned
heads
of
Europe.....

However definite an
invitation to dine . . . .

. . . and even though it is
obvious that a meal is
on the way . . . .

... a perfect lady will remain calm and apparently uninterested until the last minute............

... and greet the appearance of food with cries of delight and astonishment.

How to eat melon in polite society:

a: the right method : →

b: the wrong method: →

NEVER wipe your nose on a cleric's table napkin ...

Why ? Because it is disrespectful to the cloth....

SPOT THE MISTAKE

BELCHING: This problem can be easily disguised by converting the sudden uprush of gas from the stomach into musical sounds. Certain to startle and delight your friends.

...remember me... but ahhhhhhh! forget my fate.......

Here, a sufferer from heartburn is singing the final aria from 'Dido and Aeneas', after an unfortunate dish of radishes.

If you wish to be reinvited, follow these simple rules....

.... the Good Guest* is one who...

* guaranteed five-star by the Good Guest Guide

... adapts quickly to her surroundings...

and takes a passive role in any domestic dispute she may witness....

A Few Notes on Deportment...

← Eagerness is vulgar and should be nipped in the bud — for remember, the eager girl will become an eager woman...

In standing, the vertical → position is to be preferred. Try not to deviate by more than 10°. (it may help to imagine that your body is suspended on a string which comes out of the top of your head, and to carry a large protractor in your handbag)....

↑ Going downstairs gracefully is a problem too few women have come to terms with...

THE CURTSEY:

← a curtsey made while wearing nylon ski-pants is rarely a success.

This lady is fated to make ungraceful curtseys.
Why?
Because she has forgotten her centre of gravity.

SPOT THE MISTAKE:

This lady is making
two grave social
errors:
not only is she
pointing, she is
making a coarse
personal remark.

A Note on Nasal Hygiene.

a small reticule attached to the wrist
(or any other limb) containing a fresh
supply of pocket handkerchieves will
be most useful. It is a foolish creature
who goes unprepared to bed, and impromptu
solutions to 'nasal drip', as we doctors call it,
are rarely successful.

any lady who stoops to wiping her nasal organ
on a duvet, her own or anyone else's, will
gain a most unpleasant reputation: tongues will wag.

SPOT THE MISTAKE.

Here is a fine example of what we psychiatrists call 'Negative Social Interaction'.
The lady is breaking several taboos by: a: pointing.
b: standing on the table.
c: emasculating the male by removing his toupée.

A Word to the Wise:

'Farting', as we neurologists call it, need never distress a clever woman. Simply send away for a year's supply of Patent Floral Scented Suppositories. These, when inserted in the appropriate orifice, will relieve the most anxious of ladies. Imagine the self-assurance this invention will bring! you will be happy — nay, <u>eager</u> — to break wind in public when you know you will be wafting delightful odours of roses, violets, and lily-of-the-valley into the room, raising gasps of pleasure from all around you.

lifting the covers on .... BOUDOIR MANNERS

Boudoir modes.

What should be worn in bed? is the question on every woman's lips this season. No-one need be at fault if she observes the following rule:

if the affair is strictly <u>casual</u>, casual attire may be worn.

If it is a more formal affair, a light floral hat and gloves reaching no further than the elbow will never look out of place.

I'm not playing...

(A bishop's wife whose sense of precedence has been outraged is a joy to nobody)

Precedence in bed.

Going to bed with more than one person, or 'multiple fun' as we sociologists call it, may cause problems in etiquette.

If you are all of similar rank, maturity should rule the day. Otherwise, the order of precedence ought to be: a bishop's wife first, followed by members of any chartered profession, teachers and librarians, and lastly, discharged members of her Majesty's Forces.

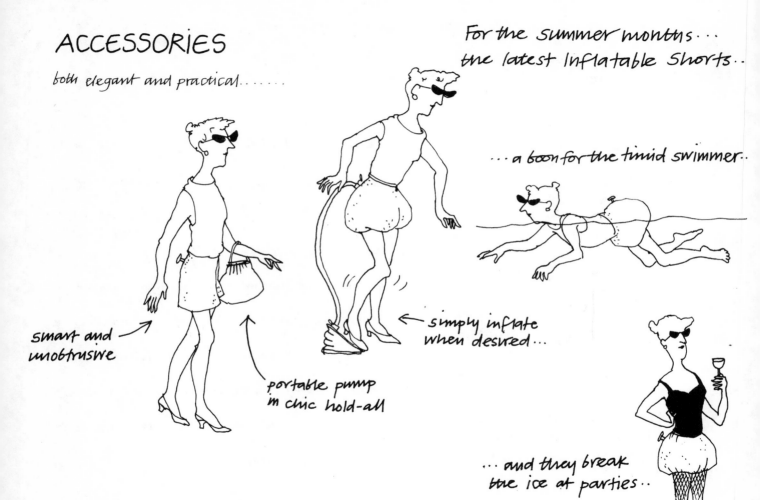

ACCESSORIES

both elegant and practical.......

For the summer months...
the latest Inflatable Shorts...

...a boon for the timid swimmer...

smart and
unobtrusive

simply inflate
when desired...

portable pump
in chic hold-all

...and they break
the ice at parties..

ARE <u>YOU</u> CURSED WITH THE CLASSIC BRITISH PEAR-SHAPED FIGURE?

Don't fancy pills, diets, or time-consuming exercises?
Simply invest in the right accessory — it makes all the difference...

an elegant solution:
The Outsize Ladies' Handbag

it covers a multitude of sins...

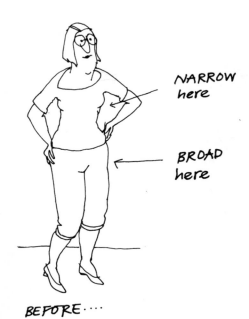

NARROW here

BROAD here

BEFORE....

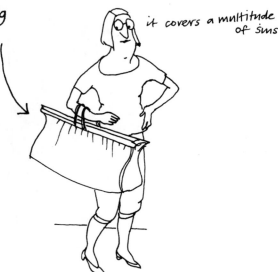

AFTER....

Why be put upon by space-invading fellow passengers on public transport?
Simply use the patent Knee-Grip, indispensable on bus, train, plane, or in the cinema...

(the patent Knee-Grip, in discreet carrier)

INSTRUCTIONS FOR USE:

1. When use of knee-grip becomes necessary, make feint karate-chop in direction of offender's vulnerable parts...

2. ...he will then take up defensive position....

3. Simply slip on clamp over hands and knees.

(complete with time-clock, can immobilise offenders for up to 24 hours.)

Here endeth etiquette...

So.....that should knock the uncouthness out of you.....
yea, even unto the third and fourth generations.......

Literary Glimpses

the accomplished
nature poet, Ethel M. Dunnock,
(M·A·OXON), author of
'Poems from My Window'
'Enchanted Hours' and
'Walks in Rural Surrey: a ramblers'
guide in free verse'......

.. two humourists on an evening off.....

Poetry as a career — a few words from our careers adviser.

...WE'RE HERE TO HELP YOU....

Considering a change of direction? Looking for a prestigious white-collar job? Why not go in for poetry? The outlay is low (and can be had for a few pence at any stationer's) and the rewards (spiritually speaking) are high.

Follow these golden rules and your success is assured:

First of all, keep fit: the slightest tendency to obesity will restrict your poetic vision (c.f. Keats' "I cannot see what flowers are at my feet...")

Further, cultivate purity of mind. Do not let long hours alone lead you into Solitary Vice. (What made Homer and Milton blind is a question too rarely asked.......)

So you wouldn't know an iambic pentameter if one fell on you? Never mind, the micro-chip revolution has made all that a thing of the past. Think <u>streamlined</u>. Pick up your pen and go . . . .

Poetry need not interfere
with everyday life.

Here, the poet is composing
while she shops, in
stout winter boots.

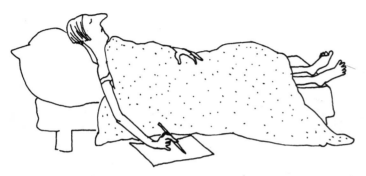

A sick poet is a bad poet...
(and no longer fashionable)

... so stay healthy — go for short, brisk walks
with a jolly companion.

(or for jolly walks with a short, brisk companion...)

Exercise those writing muscles
with a couple of hefty volumes....

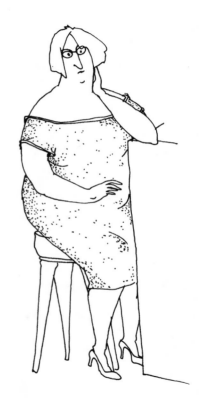

← stimuli

A really sound poet is bright-eyed, alert, and responsive to stimuli . . .

. . . a lack-lustre poet is a joy to nobody . . . . .

The Man who Mixed his Metaphors.......

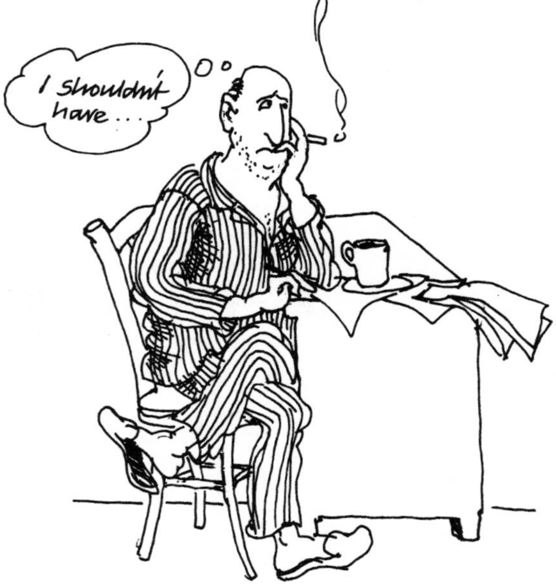

THE OCCULT....

First, why <u>you</u> should study astrology.... a few words from our resident astrologer:

1. Because it is an ancient and fascinating branch of learning, handed down to us from the time of the Babylonians.....

2. Because it gives one a Deep Insight into Human Nature ...

3. Because it is not only a science but a highly creative art....

4.... and it takes your mind off Living Under the Bomb.....

PISCES

February 20th – March 20th.

(the waitress
is obviously
a Virgo
and passing
a stern moral
judgement).

A Pisces with an afflicted Neptune who has taken to gin.

Pisces subjects take seriously not only their

own spirituality....

Dear Mrs. Gibbs,

Bernadette will not be coming to school this week as she is going through a Dark Night of the Soul......

blimey!

.... but also that of their children .....

A case of cannibalism: sentimental Pisces eating whitebait

ARIES

March 21st - april 20th

The aries woman is strong and masterful in love.....

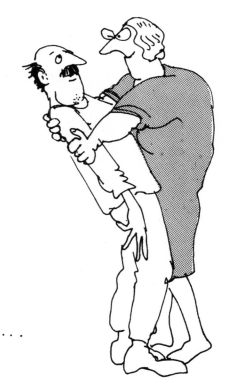

The Aries Child
(if subject to petty restrictions)
    tends to leave home
        at an early age.....

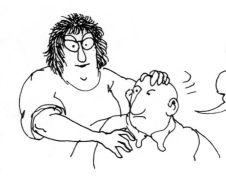

Forceful aries with stubborn capricorn:
a difficult combination.

TAURUS

april 21st – May 20th.

The Taurus child
is generally good-natured and
tractable, but has a tendency to
hoard large and unlovely objects.

all mine!

<u>strange but true</u>: many Taurean males have
the habit of picking their ears with rolled-up
bus tickets, a fact which is undergoing extensive
research at several american universities.

Even young Taureans are remarkable for their financial acumen....

Practical Taurus having trouble communicating
with an elusive Aquarian...

GEMINI
May 21st – 20th June

Gemini couples are generally happy couples, gay and sportive.

alert of mind, Geminis are
rarely vigorous in body...

...but even a Gemini
may become blocked
when Mercury is
retrograde...

Geminis, often journalists,
write fluently: those with
a strong Taurean influence, even
<u>copiously</u>....

CANCER

June 21st – July 20th

Disorganised Cancer anxiously looking for the phone she can hear ringing, but can't find....

The Cancer Male — luxurious and fastidious

LEO

July 21st – August 21st.

Leo is a generous and good-natured host, as long as she remains centre of attention...

The Forthright Leo child may wound a sensitive Cancer parent.....

VIRGO

August 22nd - September 22nd.

The Virgo child: neat, studious and anxious to please.

a 45 year old Virgo in nostalgic mood....

A Virgo with an afflicted moon will hang on to relics of an orderly past.....

**LESS
PROTEIN
LESS
PASSION**

Virgos are particular about diet —
sometimes absurdly so....

LIBRA

September 23rd – October 22nd.

Libra, elegant and musical

The Libra Child
the most civilized of
infants...

An abnormally unbalanced Libra male
(owing to a malignly aspected Mars and a high
intake of stout)

the
average
Libra,
however,
is
mild-
mannered
and
bookish

SCORPIO

October 23rd – November 22nd.

The Scorpio Child
shows from an early age its inborn tendency to suspiciousness......

intense and brooding, a badly blighted Scorpio may turn to poison pen letters, silent phone calls .... or worse ....

The Scorpio Male likes to shock...

SAGITTARIUS

November 23rd – December 20th

health-conscious virgo trying to convert a tactless Sagittarius...

A Sagittarius with a Virgo mate:
her urges for confrontation are unlikely to be
satisfied by her peace-making consort.

CAPRICORN

December 21st - January 19th

CAPRICORN

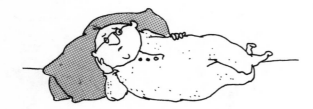

....a born worrier....

A capicorn librarian in her leisure hours.
(capicorns are much attracted to the classical)

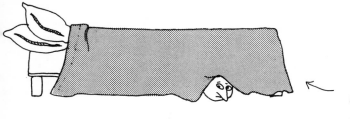

Capicorns are romantically inclined, but fear to take the initiative....

A particularly meek Capicornian male waiting for Ms. Right

AQUARIUS

January 20th - February 19th.

... and it's made
entirely of J-cloths....

(a Leo who
dislikes being
upstaged)

The easy elegance of aquarius may arouse envy
in less inventive signs...

Historical Glimpses....

(a Puritan nuclear family before the invention of the frisbee...

DID YOU KNOW······

the frisbee was invented by a woman··?

··· to wit, Patience Frisbee, of good puritan stock, one dull day in Pennsylvania 1671·····

An early stone-age frisbee
undergoing an unsuccessful trial run....

Fatal Misunderstandings in History.... a myth explained....

(* according to modern exegists, what she was really after was a tuna-fish sandwich)

A Tudor courtship . . . . .

The Language of the Fan....

I've had it up to HERE with your inane conversation...

Get me a gin and make it a big one....

... a must in the modern ballroom ....

Please change the subject ..

... an unholy bore
is approaching —
prepare for
take-off ...

WHO KNEADS THERAPY ?

The Philanthropist...

... Ever thought of voluntary work, Maria?

QUAINT BELIEFS OF THE WESTERN TRIBES

It is a common belief
among males of the
northern and western
tribes of Europe that
touching a vacuum cleaner
will make them impotent.

.... and that the presence of children in pubs makes the beer go flat....

give 'em one between the eyes...

what'll I do if they get past the door?

Ructions at Radclyffe Hall .....

.... a Gothic tale, featuring Miss Helen Highwater in the ingénue rôle....

Ructions at Radclyffe Hall...

My story begins on a dark December morning, following the funeral of my last relation on earth, Uncle Mortimer. Our trusted family solicitor broke the news....

That very evening I penned a letter of application
to an employment agency run by a certain
Mrs. Wimple, a florid widow given to the
wearing of costly jet ornaments, but
nevertheless of sound principles.....

hmm... qualified to
instruct in French,
Italian, fine sewing,
Berlin Woolwork and the
use of the Globes...
.. a likely candidate
for the Hall, if she is of
a calm and unsuperstitious
nature....

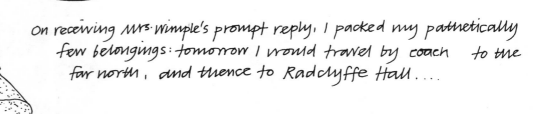

On receiving Mrs. Wimple's prompt reply, I packed my pathetically
few belongings: tomorrow I would travel by coach   to the
far north, and thence to Radclyffe Hall....

The journey next day was uneventful until, as ill luck would have it, only three miles from my destination....

He won't go no further tonight, miss. I'm afraid he's wrung his withers....

Knowing nothing of that equine malady, what could I do but believe the fellow?

There was no choice but to complete my journey on foot.....

... after an hour my journeys end came in sight .. so, this grim edifice was Radclyffe Hall....

Mrs. cannybody, the housekeeper, met me at the door, and gave me the history of the house ..
..... surprisingly quickly...

ah, here you be, Miss Helen, poor, friendless and alone...

Master and Mistress have been dead these last three years... caught him with her maid in his observatory, gave him a nasty dent in his astrolabe, she did. he never recovered, she died of grief, keep away from the East Wing on Fridays, miss, haunted, miss, breakfast is at eight ...... anything else you wish to know?

A tour of the house and its inmates followed.... the last of all was a source of amazeme
seated in the empty ball-room was the most exquisite creature
I had ever seen.......

.... No call, Miss... we just dust
her off & change her frock
now and then.....

That there's Miss Emmeline,
the daughter of the house, miss.
She were a wallflower at her
first ball three years
ago, and she's sat
there ever since,
waiting...

catatonic, the
doctor says.....

....and must I teach her
Berlin Woolwork and the
use of the Globes?

let me help you off with those wet things, ma'am...

I soon fell in with the routine of the house.

My time was pretty well occupied with the education — both spiritual and temporal — of the love children. But the servants in general were a surly, secretive lot.

A certain loneliness set in....

......apart from Mrs. Cannybody, only Jack the Footman was particularly friendly...

...one Friday night...
....awakening from troubled
dreams of the beautiful
Miss Emmeline — the cameo
profile, the classic bottle-shaped
shoulders. — I became aware of
strange sounds in the corridor...

.... stifled groans,
sighs, the clanking
of chains, the sound
of a dead weight
being dragged along,
muffled footsteps...

Sounds like it's coming from the East Wing — I shall ask Alice, the maid, tomorrow morning...

... I determined to trace the noises to their source,
rats or spirits notwithstanding ...

Pausing only to draw on a lawn chemise, a woollen binder,
a pair of whalebone stays, a pair of calico drawers
and two pairs of stout lisle stockings under my nightrail,
I hurried downstairs....

I'll soon settle their hash...

.... as I approached
the East Wing, the
sounds of discord and
general uproar grew
louder....

With pounding heart
I crept forwards....

... a dazzling sight met my eyes ...

GOINGS ON!

the ballroom was brilliantly lit & full of familiar figures ...
(and less familiar .... half the female population seemed to be there,
with Jack the only male ... or so it seemed ....)

Now all was clear...

Miss Emmeline was
reduced weekly to a
catatonic state only
by her Friday night
excesses...
Jack the Footman was Jill...

yes... every Friday the East Wing
was transformed into a haven
of sapphic delights...

Faced with this knowledge,
what could I do but what I did?...

....thereafter life took a turning in
which embroidery and Berlin woolwork
lost all their charms...

AN OCCUPATIONAL HAZARD.........

(Government health warning: cartoonists can be dangerous
and may injure your health..)